YOUR CHILD, YOUR CHOICE

Finding the Right School for Your Child

Gary R. Gruber, Ph.D.

Dedication

This book is dedicated to the parents who know and love their children and who want them to be well educated and capable of helping to make the world a better place for all.

PREFACE

You may have more school choices available to you than you previously thought possible. There are options that can be exercised for a number of good reasons, especially for those willing to dig in and do some research.

This handbook for parents is about how to make an informed choice, one based on several variables including the age and stage of your child and his or her specific needs and interests. There are numerous schools accessible for your consideration for the best match. That school may or may not be your local neighborhood school chosen only because of proximity. Convenience can certainly be figured into the equation, but it does not need to be the most important variable.

What is it that you want for your child's educational experience? One of the first things is to determine whether there is any difference between what you want for your child and what your child really needs. You must exercise care that as parents you do not impose expectations on your child that are either unrealistic or unreasonable.

It is reasonable to expect that your child has the capacity to develop the skills and to acquire an education that will help him or her be a productive member of a community as well as a happy and successful individual. It is also incumbent upon parents to zero in on your child's strengths and capitalize on those to help develop the hidden talents that exist within every child.

One of my former colleagues, an outstanding, long-time college counselor and author of *The College Admissions Mystique*, Bill Mayher, says that we should be in the business of creating happy 35 year-olds. As a parent of three children and stepparent of four, all of whom are now beyond 35, I appreciate Bill's point more than ever.

The educational journey needs to have a vision that extends beyond one year or even four years and includes many experiences beyond the walls of a school. You do not need to be too concerned about short-term effects from moment to moment because learning is cumulative over time and education is a process, not an event.

I believe we should also dispel the myth that everyone needs to go to college, especially a four-year, post secondary college or university that is theoretically supposed to guarantee a good job and a better life. There are many viable, post-secondary training experiences that do not require a four year or even in some cases a two year commitment. These avenues include technology, electronics, skilled mechanics and engineering, and apprenticeships in a variety of trades or as a creative and innovative entrepreneur.

Today, a bachelor's degree at the expense of four years of one's life and considerable cost guarantees very little. It remains however, the pre-requisite, in most cases, to do graduate work in a university. Local community colleges have risen in the ranks of a quality post-secondary education and they are much more affordable than many other colleges.

For those of us who are committed life-long learners there are always new things to learn. We can explore fields outside our own professional experiences in a continuing curiosity about the world and the people who populate it. And for some, taking a course that is unrelated to our sometimes more narrow concentration has been a real pleasure and joy.

As an example, I know an engineer who took a woodworking course and although he was familiar with tools of his current trade, woodworking was an entirely new and enjoyable experience. Another example closer to home is when I took a course in my undergraduate university in residential architecture. That learning experience stimulated an interest in architecture and design that continues to this day.

What most parents seem to want, regardless of where they live or their socio-economic status is exemplified by a quote from a film, fourteen years in the making. *American Promise,* by Michele Stephenson and Joe Brewster, documents their son's and his best friend's educational experiences at an elite private school in New York City:

"...parents want their children to acquire a sense of self-esteem and self-determination. And every permutation of the academic experience (single sex/coed, public/private/charter,

3

racially diverse and downtown, or socioeconomically stratified uptown) is presented as some grand experiment that might reveal 'The Solution' to growing exceptional children, as if such a thing exists."

As parents you want your children to be motivated, to be engaged in meaningful learning experiences and to have solid relationships with their teachers that are positive, supportive and inspiring. You want your children to be able to relate successfully to other children who may well come from different backgrounds as this is what they will encounter in the larger world. Perhaps most of all, you want your children to believe in themselves and their self-worth such that they know they are capable of being successful in whatever they choose to do. They will need this sense of themselves as they take on more and more responsibility for their own choices and their future life and work.

Happy are those parents whose children look forward to going to school every day and being immersed and absorbed in learning and in those things that most schools want them to learn. Some of the stated priorities from good schools include critical thinking, problem solving, self-expression, creativity and a continuing curiosity about the world and themselves. Many schools also emphasize the importance of being a compassionate, good citizen both in the school community and the larger neighborhood. In many schools, the importance of giving something back through community service is emphasized in one or more ways.

At the end of the day when you pose the classic question, "What did you do at school today?" the most desirable response you can hear is something that includes genuine enthusiasm around what is happening that keeps children engaged in a dialogue about learning. It is not just about the acquisition of knowledge but about how to apply what is being learned and which experiences are bolstering the student's confidence in taking more responsibility for his or her own continuing educational journey.

You might think about re-phrasing the question to "What is the most interesting thing you learned at school today? Or "Tell me something you learned today that you think I might not know." This will convey to your child that you are genuinely interested in what's going on at school.

As a parent you also want your child to be challenged to take intelligent risks, to venture into new experiences and try a variety of different things. The old cookie cutter approach to education of trying to make a child fit into a prescribed program has not worked very well for most children.

You should be trying to find a program that fits your child and his or her needs. Too much of the "one size fits all" approach has resulted in students losing interest in learning, and they become bored, frustrated and disappointed with their school experiences. That is obviously not a very good formula for being happy for a successful academic experience.

NOTES:

Chapter One

YOUR CHILD

There is a large amount of diversity among children, each with different needs, different abilities, different interests, different personalities, and different challenges. Your child is unique, *one of a kind*. Yes, there are similarities between and among children but the distinguishing features are what make your child who he or she is.

We begin with your child (or children) and the belief that each one is unique and while there may be similarities according to what Sir Ken Robinson calls "their date of manufacture" why should that be the only thing they have in common when they go to school? Most schools are not organized to deal with individual students as unique human beings. Thus we have had mass production delivering education along the lines of an industrial model of factory education for much too long.

We crank them out in batches and move them along the assembly line of grade levels. We then add the necessary parts along the way to try and make them function successfully and we often pressure them to perform at the highest levels. We test them for quality control and their scores are used to determine all kinds of things including whether or not the factory is producing good models. This entire experience can produce both fear and stress responses which impede the learning process greatly. Perhaps those impediments are obvious to any keen observer. If you have not seen Ken Robinson's illustrated video lecture, be sure to look it up on You Tube. This short presentation makes the case very clear.

Let's start with *your* child and see what we can understand and appreciate that will help us determine how best to meet his or her needs within the context of an optimal educational experience. We will look at the different ages and stages of children in the K-12 range and see how the periods of growth and change correlate with different grade levels in the school experience.

You may have heard the comment attributed to Mark Twain that he never let schooling interfere with his education. What we can conclude from his remark is that school should enhance and enrich learning and *not* present obstacles that must be overcome. Instead of schools' testing to find a child's weaknesses and mistakes, time and energy might be better spent testing to find and capitalize on a child's strengths.

This is not to say that areas of weakness should not be identified and overcome but rather that a child is much more likely to grow, prosper and succeed by focusing on what the child likes and does well as opposed to the opposite.

When school is either too difficult or too boring, a child can lose interest and disengage quickly. There is often as much or more learning that can take place *outside* of school, as we know it. We can look at the rise in the number of students who are home schooled as evidence of this phenomenon.

Three percent of American students between the ages of 5-17, about 1.5 million children are home schooled, according to the *2012 Statistical Abstract* released by the U.S. Census Bureau. That number has increased steadily over the past several years. The main reason given by parents who home school their children is their disagreement with some aspect of the school environment. There are other reasons given such as disagreement with a style of teaching or issues with the curriculum, but the learning environment is perhaps the most important factor in any child's educational experience.

Home schooling is one option that may be appropriate to keep in mind and may be considered along with other, more traditional approaches. Much may depend on where you live and what school choices are available in your specific geographical area. If you add a boarding school to the myriad of choices, a residential school may increase the number of your choices.

Children grow and develop according to a well-studied and well-researched scheme of maturation from birth through adolescence into adulthood. During that time, since most children begin school with kindergarten around age 5, they spend upwards of 1500 hours per year in school, including homework. In thirteen years, that totals 19,500 hours or approximately 2,438 eight-hour days! Add to those numbers both a pre-school experience and summer school and the hours and days are increased significantly. In order to have an excellent return on the investment of time, you can understand why it is so important that all this time invested needs to be in the best possible place for your child.

The Early Years

In the early years, from ages 2-5, a number of developments are unfolding that are critical to a child's healthy growth. When a child begins to walk on his or her own, a new phase in development begins. At this stage children can now explore their world on their own. They want to discover what their environment is all about. Their ability to express themselves through language takes giant steps as they learn to give names to objects of interest and to ask for things as they realize their independent nature. And yes, they develop the facility to say *"No!"*

At this developmental stage, parents often experience the challenge of helping a child develop some emotional regulation. "Meltdowns" are common during this time and parents need to know how to use the bond developed during infancy to help the child learn to regulate their emotional expression and at least begin to grasp the difficult concept of delayed gratification. While toddlers instinctively seem to be able to say "No" they also need help in learning how to accept "No" from others. Difficult? Yes! Impossible? No!

What your child needs at this juncture is consistency that he or she can count on. Children need a response that fits within the structure of your agreed upon family's values and some well-defined boundaries and limits. They need also to know what lies beyond, in the uncharted and unknown territory. This can also be the beginning of the choice/consequence process when your child learns that a good choice has good results and a poor choice has undesirable results.

Consequence is synonymous with result although most children come to believe that a consequence is most often *negative*. It is important to keep these things in mind when reviewing a school that fits with your kind of discipline or at least discipline with which you agree wholeheartedly and can support enthusiastically. Discipline is not synonymous with punishment but rather with learning. This may be surprising, but in fact, the origin of the word *discipline* is related to the word *disciple*, or someone who follows a teacher. However, through common usage it has morphed into meaning harsh training or punishment that is supposed to be corrective and instructive. It is at least clear that discipline has to do with rules and expectations for desirable behavior as well as the results when the rules aren't followed.

It is acceptable, even desirable for children to make mistakes, as these minor errors are opportunities for learning. It is better to make mistakes or fail when it is least costly and then learn sufficiently from the experiences so as not to repeat the same mistakes later. George Santayana is credited with the saying, "Those who do not learn from their mistakes are doomed to repeat them."

The early years are also a time for parents to take advantage of a spurt in physical and intellectual development and help your children get ready to begin their school experience for the first time. An important part of school includes interacting cooperatively with others while at the same time being able to compete on the same level physically, intellectually socially and emotionally. Consequently, it does not make much sense to group children by age alone since they may be at different levels of development within an age range. Children grow and change at different times and at different rates, some faster, some slower.

The old one-room schoolhouse is a good illustration of how multi-age groupings can and do work. There are numerous, successful international models of multi-age classrooms in the Netherlands, Finland, Western Australia and Canada. Multi-age programs do not compare children and instead consider the uniqueness of each learner in terms of learning rate, background, learning styles, multiple intelligences and interests. States do not track multi-age classrooms in terms of comparisons but there have been good examples, especially in Alaska and Kentucky. Montessori schools are also known for early years multi-age groupings.

Multi-age does not try to fit a child to a pre-determined curriculum but instead chooses a broad-based curriculum to fit the needs and interests of the child. Schools are slow to adopt this model because it does not fit a curriculum sequenced by grade, grade level tests and scores, and the rather rigid, inflexible, one-size fits all NCLB (No Child Left Behind) model.

As the child's parent, you are in the position of being the one to provide the right combination of encouragement, support and guidance. You can also serve as their first teacher to help master some basic learning skills and you can have active discussions and experiments with these new concepts and skills.

This is why it is so important for you to read to your children from an early age onward. It can be similarly productive to engage in other activities with numbers, drawing and painting, singing and dancing, pointing out objects in nature as well as taking part in events in your local community. These can all be age appropriate activities according to your child's interest and response and it's a good way to introduce your children to a wide variety of choices.

Another important point to remember is that structured and unstructured physical movement is part of any good school program. Recent research in gender studies suggests it may be more necessary for boys than for girls although it is clear that both boys and girls benefit from the experience. Too many teachers (and schools) have expected children to sit still and be quiet and that flies squarely in the face of what children need. They need to be active and moving as part of their development and to stifle that movement, stifles learning.

In the early years and grades, much of what might look like play can actually be serious learning experiences, developing fine motor skills and hand-eye coordination by using pencils, pens, brushes, scissors, and garden tools where possible. Learning to make things work and seeing the results can help enormously to reinforce a love of learning for its own sake as well as for the outcome. It is even possible to learn how to overcome frustration and disappointment when something doesn't work the first time!

Play: How It Shapes the Brain, Opens the Imagination, and Invigorates the Soul, a book by Stuart Brown, psychiatrist and Associate Professor at UCSD in San Diego is a terrific guide to understanding the importance of play in developing a child's innate interests and talents. We need to understood the value of what looks like play in children and how important it is for continuing to help a child evolve and discover so much more about who he or she really is and what they are about.

These early years are critical but there should be no rush to push your child to get ahead out of fear of being left behind. There is more than enough parental anxiety about your child's growth and development without manufacturing more! Relax and have fun with your children. They will remember the quality time you spent with them more than whether or not your house and kitchen were models of spotless perfection, or that you spent extra hours at a job outside of home in order to give your family additional material goods. In many cases it may be necessary for one or both parents to work outside the home and providing quality time with your children during non-working hours becomes even more critical.

NOTES:

School Age Years

The "school age" years of 6-12 are extremely rich as the mental, physical, emotional and social aspects of your child begin to evolve, develop and take a big step forward. There is an abundance of literature in the child development field that describes what is going on during these years. The following outline of growth and change in children from ages 6-12 is an excellent summary from the Stanford Children's Health Department connected with the Lucille Packard Children's Hospital in California.

What can your child do at this age?

As your child continues to grow, you will notice new and exciting abilities that your child develops. While children may progress at different rates and have diverse interests, the following are some of the common milestones children may reach in this age group:
- 6 to 7 year-olds:
    - Enjoys many activities and stays busy
    - Likes to paint and draw
    - May lose first tooth
    - Vision is as sharp as an adult's vision
    - Practices skills in order to become better
    - Jumps rope
    - Rides a bike
- 8 to 9 year-olds:
    - More graceful with movements and abilities
    - Jumps, skips, and chases

- Dresses and grooms self completely
- Can use tools (i.e., hammer, screwdriver)

•

- 10 to 12 year-olds:
  - Remainder of adult teeth will develop
  - Likes to sew and paint

What does your child understand?

As children enter into school age, their abilities and understanding of concepts and the world around them continue to grow. While children may progress at different rates, the following are some of the common milestones children may reach in this age group:

- 6 to 7 year-olds:
  - Understands concept of numbers
  - Knows daytime and nighttime
  - Knows right and left hands
  - Can copy complex shapes, such as a diamond
  - Can tell time
  - Can understand commands with three separate instructions
  - Can explain objects and their use
  - Can repeat three numbers backwards
  - Can read age-appropriate books and/or materials
- 8 to 9 year-olds:
  - Can count backwards

- o Knows the date
- o Reads more and enjoys reading
- o Understands fractions
- o Understands concept of space
- o Draws and paints
- o Can name months and days of week, in order
- o Enjoys collecting objects
- 10 to 12 year-olds:
  - o Writes stories
  - o Likes to write letters
  - o Reads well
  - o Enjoys using the telephone

How does your child interact with others?

A very important part of growing up is the ability to interact and socialize with others. During the school-age years, you will see a transition in your child as he or she moves from playing alone to having multiple friends and social groups. While friendships become more important, the child is still fond of his or her parents and likes being part of a family. While every child is unique and will develop different personalities, the following are some of the common behavioral traits that may be present in your child:
- 6 to 7 year-olds:
  - o Cooperates and shares
  - o Jealous of others and siblings
  - o Likes to copy adults

- Likes to play alone, but friends are becoming important
- Plays with friends of the same gender
- May have temper tantrums
- Modest about body
- Likes to play board games
- 8 to 9 year-olds:
  - Likes competition and games
  - Starts to mix friends and play with children of the opposite gender
  - Modest about body
  - Enjoys clubs and groups, such as Boy Scouts or Girl Scouts
  - Becoming interested in boy-girl relationships, but does not admit it
- 10 to 12 year-olds:
  - Friends are very important; may have a best friend
  - Increased interest in the opposite gender
  - Likes and respects parents
  - Enjoys talking to others

How to help increase your school-aged child's social ability

Consider the following as ways to foster your school-aged child's social abilities:
- Set and provide appropriate limits, guidelines, and expectations and consistently enforce using appropriate consequences.

- Model appropriate behavior.
- Offer compliments for your child being cooperative and for any personal achievements.
- Help your child choose activities that are appropriate for your child's abilities.
- Encourage your child to talk with you and be open with his or her feelings.
- Encourage your child to read and read with your child.
- Encourage your child to get involved with hobbies and other activities.
- Encourage physical activity.
- Encourage self-discipline; expect your child to follow rules that are set.
- Teach your child to respect and listen to authority figures.
- Encourage your child to talk about peer pressure and help set guidelines to deal with peer pressure.
- Spend uninterrupted time together—giving full attention to your child.
- Limit television, video, and computer time

NOTES:

The importance of parental participation and support

Research increasingly points to the importance of developing social and emotional skills along with the cognitive and physical abilities so often promoted as being the more important ones for moving on to a higher level. Your help, encouragement and support with developing these abilities will set the stage for a most successful school experience, at least in most schools. You want your child to be well prepared for these first six or seven years of school.

The first several years and grades of school, from about age 5 or 6 to 11 or 12, consist of laying a solid foundation and acquiring many of the basic skills that will be needed later for success in almost all areas. These skills include not only reading, writing, and computation (math) but also some attention to reinforcing creativity, collaboration and cooperation. Any good school program will also have opportunities for the fine and performing arts including drawing, painting, music, dance and drama. It might not be called dance per se but perhaps "movement" of various types, especially in the first several years of school.

We should note here how often children today are "plugged in" whether to tablets, pads, and computers or other electronic devices and how this may be affecting their development whether mentally, socially, physically or emotionally. We do not yet have the research regarding the long-term effects and how it is changing how children (and adults) see the world. Suffice to say that education is scrambling to take advantage of technology and trying to do it in ways that are positive and productive.

Using computers and electronic tablets is now quite common in the early grades as children learn via technology how to access information, design projects, communicate with others, share the results of their work through various media and even develop their own programs for solving problems. As one example, students can now have access to high-powered geographical information system software that enables detailed mapping and analysis of data.

Children are certainly connected differently to each other and the rest of the world through technology, for better or for worse, and the choices that they make regarding the use and sometimes overuse of it and dependency on it can affect their learning experiences in various ways. Technology can enhance learning or it may be an escape from learning. What is important is to use technology in appropriate and constructive ways.

Schools, libraries, adults and children, now have access to information in unprecedented ways such that the old question and answer process has changed forever. Whether or not the answer is correct and whether it has any depth or background or provides any real understanding is another matter.

We have come to a point where a lot of people believe that *more, faster and bigger* are better. Competition in many situations seems out of control and cooperation has been sidelined in favor of winning. It may be unfortunate that the U.S. Dept of Education chose "Race to the Top" for their latest effort at rewarding innovation. It sounds more political than it does educational. "Love to Learn" or at least something that sounds more connected to children and teaching and learning might have been a better choice.

In many instances, *slow* still has a certain value that cannot be supplanted mechanically. Just because it "looks like a tomato" does not mean what it used to mean. GMO's, (Genetically Modified Organisms) have altered our earlier experience of what is real. We might want to encourage children to look into the purpose and value of GMO's and ask some penetrating and probing questions about a host of other products and materials.

This stage of growth and development, commonly referred to as "school age" does not need to be rushed or hurried along like a GMO tomato. This is an amazing time when the foundation is laid for much of the more advanced learning and growth that take place later.

This is the time when children develop a love of learning, or they don't. It is when they love their teachers, or they don't. It is when they like going to school and being in school, or they don't. And it is when they discover that they have the ability to make things work to their advantage, or they become discouraged because things aren't working to their advantage but rather to their disadvantage. If the latter is the case, it's time for intervention and help.

It is not necessarily an either "they like it" or "they don't" proposition because in most situations there will be some days that will not be as good as others. What we hope for is that the good days far outweigh any bad ones and that the overall experience is positive, stimulating, encouraging and supportive. We want also for their education to be challenging and inspiring and take them to new levels of learning and engagement.

 Well-equipped parents can be excellent "coaches" for your child no matter what the endeavor. Don't hesitate to ask for help when you might need it and remember that early intervention is better than waiting until a situation grows worse and much more serious.

Children like to experiment, especially with something new and different, and while it is unreasonable to keep introducing new things continually, being able to get away from too much canned and repetitious activity can keep a child engaged more easily. This is also an opportunity for teaching children to finish something they have started, taking a project to completion and having the satisfaction and reward of a job well done.

As parents of school age children, you can be in for a most wonderful time. Watching your children try new activities, cheering them on at athletic events and applauding their accomplishments at recitals are often some of the high points for parents. However, achieving success is often preceded with frustration and sometimes learning to accept one's weaknesses as will as celebrating and building on strengths.

Well-equipped parents can be excellent "coaches" for your child no matter what the endeavor. Don't hesitate to ask for help when you might need it and remember that early intervention is better than waiting until a situation grows worse and much more serious.

NOTES:

Adolescence

There are numerous resources that provide an in-depth look at this stage of child and human development. Our purpose here is to look at this period of growth in the context of the school experience, not to lay out all of the issues, both positive and negative, regarding a healthy and productive experience for your teen-agers. There are important topics during this time that include the enormous physical, mental, emotional and social changes that take place over some five to seven years between the ages of 11 and 17.

How these changes affect your children also affect their relationships with peers, with the adults in their lives and with the larger community. From academic, artistic and athletic performances to social relationships, this period of time shapes and influences what comes next. Thus it is important to pay attention to the behaviors, both desirable and undesirable, in order to better understand how, as parents, you might contribute to an optimum experience for your children both in school and otherwise.

In 1988, I wrote a book with a colleague, Bill Wingerd, called *Understanding and Enjoying Adolescence*. (Longman, 1988) Our premise was that if you could understand that stage of growth and development better, both you and your child could enjoy it more. It was in print for 10 years and if you are interested you can probably still find it. Much has definitely changed in the world since then but many of the individual aspects, especially physical, emotional and social, have remained somewhat constant in spite of all the trappings surrounding them.

Ages 11-17 – Do not get hung up on a precise age. Some children start early, some are late bloomers and there are several growth variables at work in terms of rate of growth and change. Genetics play a role as do hormones, diet and physical condition. Some children become much more independent earlier, others later. There is room for a lot of individual differences within a particular age group during this stage of growth, one primarily marked by change. It is said that more change takes place during these years than at any other time in a child's life with one exception and that is during the first nine months in utero.

There are two groups within this larger one, the early adolescent years, sometimes in a "middle" school environment and the later adolescent years usually in a "high" school. I have often eschewed the lower, middle, and upper terms in favor of primary or elementary. I prefer the term secondary to high school as the implication is that higher is better and more desirable. It's surprising that we haven't discovered a higher and highest school! Perhaps we have unwittingly done so with college and graduate school as the higher and highest domains! We have been stuck with that nomenclature for much too long. I doubt that the names of most school environments will change yet there is much to be said in a name that can be descriptive of the experience.

At the beginning of each of these two groups of years, at age 11 and then again around age 14, there may come a point in time where you may wish to consider whether or not to continue in a particular school or to consider a change.

Some schools actually end in either grade 5 or grade 6, depending on the configurations of schools in your local area. There may be some K-12 schools, mostly in the private arena, and while that is a long time to be in one school environment the experience changes along the way for many reasons. There are different buildings, different teachers, different students entering and leaving and of course, different programs of study and activities.

Many middle schools in the public domain are stand alone schools for grades 5 or 6 through grades 8 or 9 and then there are the final three or four years in a high school, upper school. In the private arena, many middle schools are either the higher grades in a K-8 school or the lower grades in a 6-12 school. It really is the experience that counts, not the labels, or even the ages or grades.

Speaking of labels, I want to offer a note regarding the negative effects of labeling children (or adults for that matter.) We are often too eager to tack a name onto a child and his or her behavior whether positive or negative and you can think of many. Here are a few: slow, gifted, ADD, ADHD, impulsive, compulsive, obsessive, fixated, learning disabled, dyslexic, disadvantaged, privileged, rude, rowdy, destructive, loud, unmanageable, difficult, calm, sweet, easy going, well-behaved, polite, focused, compliant, defiant, physically challenged and so on. The list of names and labels is endless. Some are diagnostic in nature and may result in prescribed medication and that can be a challenge in and of itself, to be sure that the medication is managed well and kept in an appropriate balance.

What we do, often unintentionally, is to set up expectations for the child as well as the adults dealing with the child, that a diagnosis provides an explanation of obstacles that must be dealt with if the child is to make progress in most school environments. Even a compliant child who is easy might not be willing to take any risks and underneath all of the desirable and positive behavior is a really quite insecure person lacking in confidence, not a good recipe for later success. It is much better to understand what lies behind the behavior rather than see the behavior as the problem.

These so-called "middle years" signal a greater degree of independence, experimentation and more choices. Your child is finding his or her own voice, one that is separate from yours and at times it may seem as if he or she is being disagreeable just for the sake of an argument. It may not be the classic rebellion against authority but rather an honest attempt to make a decision that the child wants to at least try out and see how it fits. You may believe that because you know more and you know whether or not there is a greater or lesser likelihood for success that you can protect your child and prevent a mistake. That said, it is also possible to learn a lot from mistakes, especially if they are not too costly.

Among many other challenges, your child is trying to navigate through two very important channels at the same time during these early adolescent years and neither channel is without challenges and, at times, disappointments. This can also be a time to discover more talents, skills and strengths on which we can capitalize to make this part of the journey a bit easier and more pleasant.

The two channels are the relationships on one hand with friends, both boys and girls, and on the other hand, relationships with adults, especially teachers, parents of friends and friends of one's own parents. Coaches, advisors, neighbors and other adults may also be role models in helping a child want to emulate someone other than parents. Remember that your child is trying to create distance from you and become independent and you might think it's too soon.

Growing up and becoming independent is a process over time, and not an event marked by a birthday. However, cultural and religious celebrations such as confirmations and bar and bas mitzvahs are tied to a "coming of age" meaning closer to adulthood and the responsibilities associated with it. There are numerous rites of passage that can be celebrated within the context of family or school that can send a clear signal about accepting adult responsibility. One more example is a driver's license which comes with enormous responsibilities and is a privilege which can easily be removed.

You can see why it is important that you choose a school for these middle years where you have confidence in the adults who are there. They will be the ones interacting with your child as a lot of the adult influence will shift from you to their teachers. You will always be the parent and you will always be there. It is important to let your children know that in different ways and to also let them know that you are willing to change your position and become more of a coach, manager and advisor than the absolute and final authority. It will be a relief to your child, and perhaps to you too, for you to relinquish some of the previously held authority thus paving the way for a continuing positive relationship.

What you want to look for in a middle school environment is one that is safe for a child to be an individual and in a place where a child will not feel threatened or insecure because of differences in physical, emotional and intellectual expressions. These can be awkward years in terms of growth, as well as comfort with self and others.

Bullying has been a recent topic of concern in many places. It is important to know what the school's policies and practices are with regard to respect for individual differences. In addition to personality and behavioral differences I would also emphasize that you understand how a school deals with race, religion, ethnicity, gender, sexual identity, sexual preferences, and socio-economic class.

The academic, artistic and athletic offerings of middle schools vary greatly. Depending on your child' particular needs and interests, you need to be as certain as possible that this experience will enhance and enrich your child's overall learning and social experience. You want your happy child to have many more good days than bad ones. It is not the end of the world to have a bad day now and then, everyone does, but if there is a pattern of negative experiences or if you child does not seem engaged in meaningful ways, that is sufficient reason to be concerned.

The high school years, usually defined as grades 9 or 10 through grade 12, consist of a variety of programs with numerous choices and concentrations. These grades offer different course selections and there are often counselors to help choose from among these offerings. There may be different levels of basic academic courses based on your child's abilities. There should also be offerings in the fine and performing arts, different athletic programs whether inter-scholastic competition or intramural, and recreational activities.

The point here is to aim for a well-rounded experience that includes many opportunities for individual expression through a variety of different experiences. Narrowing the choices and concentrating in only one area too early may prevent a child from experiencing something that might lead to an interest yet undiscovered and untapped. The point is not to prevent a passionate interest from being developed further but to be reasonably sure that there is a wide exposure to a variety of opportunities.

Nurturing a passion for learning new things can open doors to possibilities that may not have been considered previously. Sometimes a specific course or experience, or working with a particular teacher, can be the inspiration that will propel a student beyond what was earlier thought possible.

Along with the academic, artistic and athletic experiences of these years come the many social experiments in which most students engage. Friends seem to dominate the social scene with constant communication including instant text messages which tend to be the order of the day. icated

Which school will serve your child best will depend on a number of variables that include your child's adaptation to a new environment and how much emphasis the school places on understanding the individual needs of each child. While many schools will say that they provide individually designed programs and successful students, the evidence can be found by talking with other parents and by looking carefully at the school and the students who are there. What you are looking for are happy parents, happy students and indications that genuine learning is enjoyable, exciting and ongoing.

NOTES:

Chapter Two

THE SCHOOL

There are many different kinds of schools that include the following:

- Public schools, those which the majority of students in the United States attend;
- Charter schools, also public schools that must be selected;
- Magnet schools, also public schools, with a particular emphasis and focus;
- Private schools, both proprietary and non-profit independent schools. These are not in the public domain.

We will consider different types of schools to understand the larger picture and where you might fit in according to your preferences and those of your child. All of this assumes that you have a choice and we believe that an informed choice will serve you and your children better than a simple automatic response without serious consideration. You may not have previously thought that you could choose the school where your child would be best served. My objective is to open the door for you to consider more possibilities.

As early as 1990, John Chubb and Terry Moe, at a think tank in Washington, D.C., researched and wrote a book called *Politics, Markets and America's Schools*. They recommended a new system of public education, built around parent-student choice and school competition. They believed that this kind of system would promote school autonomy thus providing a firm foundation for genuine school improvement and superior student achievement.

There has not been much competition in the public arena but parents' abilities to make choices about where their students will attend school have increased significantly. This recent trend has spurred more competition and improvement than previously when schools were left on their own to improve themselves. That seldom happened.

A prime example is in the charter school movement where the per capita funds for each student goes with the student wherever the student goes to school. That is one reason charter schools have been controversial with many teachers' unions and with those school districts that have been opposed to them. Loss of revenue to the public systems meant less money for the personnel and programs as they were currently structured and school systems are slow to adapt and change. Public school administrations and teacher unions seemed more interested in maintaining the status quo than in making any significant changes. However, there are signs that the climate is changing with much more cooperation on the horizon.

The National Center for Education Statistics, the primary federal entity for collecting and analyzing data related to education, reports that in the fall of 2013 about 50 million students headed off to approximately 99,000 public elementary and secondary schools. Before the school year was over, an estimated *$591 billion* were spent related to the education of these students. These funds come from federal, state and local sources mainly in the form of tax revenues, thus the myth of "free" public education.

Of these 50 million students, over 35 million were in prekindergarten through 8th grade and almost 15 million were in grades 9 through 12. An additional 5 million students were expected to attend private schools or approximately 10% of the population. And, approximately 80% of private schools have some kind of religious affiliation, primarily Roman Catholic.

Over 1 million children were expected to attend public prekindergarten in the fall of 2013. Enrollment in public kindergarten was projected to reach almost 4 million students   That fall, about 4 million public school students were expected to enroll in 9th grade, the typical entry grade for many American high schools.

The estimated cost per student in public schools, all expenses considered, was pegged right around $11,800 of taxpayer monies. The average tuition in all K-12 private schools was approximately the same and that cost is paid in a variety of ways from personal income, from scholarships and from discounted tuitions. The range of private school tuitions varies greatly according to type and size of school, as do the resources available to support the students and families who attend those schools.

Public schools are best defined as the neighborhood school where the vast majority of students attend, regardless of grade level. They are usually part of a public school district and whether a large urban district serving thousands of students, a suburban district or a very small rural district with only one or two schools, public schools have been the backbone of American public education.

By 1918, all states had a policy of mandatory or compulsory education and while it began early in the Bay Colony of Massachusetts in 1642, the compulsory piece varied from state to state.

The first private school in the United States was Collegiate School in New York City, founded in 1628 followed later in the 17th century by the founding of three Quaker schools in Philadelphia. Many well-established private schools, including those started by Catholic religious orders, especially the Jesuits and Sisters of the Sacred Heart, have a long and rich history. There are other religiously affiliated schools in addition to Catholic schools led by various orders of priests, nuns and parishes. There are a number of Protestant, church affiliated schools, Jewish schools and a much smaller percentage of Quaker and Buddhist schools. Almost all of these faith-based schools are open to all religions although some of the more conservative and evangelical, religious schools may be more narrowly defined.

Public schools are organized in a somewhat hierarchical fashion and have had to deal with teachers' unions although they seem to have become less adversarial and more cooperative in recent years. The NEA (National Education Association) and AFT (American Federation of Teachers) have formed a partnership with each other and developed a list of common goals and common projects designed to improve the quality of public education in the United States. Negotiations between the unions and the school districts have seen fewer teacher strikes and less strident demands, as management and labor appear to be working together on behalf of the children and families whom they serve.

Most public school districts have a CEO a chief executive officer known as a Superintendent who oversees the COO's, chief operating officers, known as Principals who in turn lead, manage and supervise a local school, its curriculum and the teachers. In larger districts there are many departments and many people who administer them.

Some large school districts appear to be rather complex and bureaucratic in their operations with what often appears to be a top-heavy administration. It behooves the public who is paying taxes to ask some probing questions about how school budgets are allocated and where the money goes that supports the education of their children. Anywhere from 60% to 70% percent of a school's budget in both the public and the private sectors goes toward teacher compensation. In a market or business that is heavily dependent upon the quality of the personnel that is not at all unusual or unreasonable. However, there are other expenses, both administrative and programmatic, that could be legitimately questioned as to their benefits to children.

Within the realm of public schools, there are many different kinds of schools. The advent of charter schools, beginning in 1992, produced a whole new breed of schools however, not without controversy. The best description of a charter school is that it is a *public school of choice*. However, that said, the choice is often limited by a lottery since more people have generally wanted to attend than the specific school is able to accommodate.

Experienced educators, teachers and administrators, who are often described as creative, innovative and entrepreneurial, have started many charter schools. They often felt constricted by their previous positions and jumped at the opportunity to start something fresh and new that would facilitate their vision of a meaningful education in the 21st century.

Funds for charter schools have come primarily from their per capita allocations per student, from the local district, and therein was part of the conflict or controversy as public districts began to "lose" money and students. Many charter schools started separate, charitable foundations to help fund their schools and now many public schools and districts have similar organizations to provide additional grants for their work.

The competition for the philanthropic dollar devoted to education has never been greater. Private schools, along with other non-profit organizations, began receiving charitable, tax-deductible gifts and grants in 1917, when the tax law was enacted. These contributions augment school programs and facilities and are a relatively new addition in the public arena.

Those additional funds may be earmarked for specific programs or an endowment fund. They are often created to insure future funding whether for financial assistance at tuition paying schools, additional or earmarked monies for faculty compensation or extra-curricular programs. Such activities may extend to travel opportunities, athletics, the arts and technology.

Depending upon the legislation that authorizes charter schools, various states have different requirements. One study analyzed charter school state laws in terms of two general dimensions:

1) The flexibility, freedom and support extended in the law, and

2) The degree of public accountability required of charter schools by the state

The number of charter schools in any given state varies accordingly. Those states that have the greatest flexibility in establishing charter schools also having the greatest number of charter schools from which to choose. Somewhat surprisingly, most of these states also demand the most accountability.

California has the highest number of students attending charter schools and while approximately 7% of California students attend charter schools, the percentage at a national level has increased to almost 13%. There are numerous reasons for the steady growth of charter schools both in number and quality. Many educators see charter schools offering more freedom and flexibility in designing and delivering education for both students and teachers.

California also has the highest number of charter schools of any state in the country with 1,130 schools serving over half a million students as of the fall of 2013. In 2013-14, 104 new charter schools opened in California. For the 2012-13 school year, there were almost 50,000 students on charter school wait lists. This includes more than 15,000 students on wait lists in Los Angeles Unified School District.

Since 1995, the number of charter schools in Arizona has grown to over 500 and charter school student enrollment has grown well over 113,000 students, accounting for 10% of the student population in Arizona. There are currently 208 charters operating in New York State, 183 of which are located in New York City and a waiting list of some 45,000 students. It is quite obvious that charter schools are seen as viable choices and the demand is greater than the supply.

One of the many challenges facing public schools is that because school is mandatory for all children, those schools must provide an education for all students regardless of their needs or the costs. While these resources must be made available, they can also be very costly, especially if you have to have a single, experienced, well-trained teacher for two or three special needs students. States and local judicatories must pay for these resources by providing the facilities and personnel to meet the needs of these students including the high cost of transportation, usually by buses provided by the school district.

The expenses mount up quickly and thus far, there has been very few creative solutions to the challenges of financial sustainability. The cost per student in these situations can be three or four times the cost per student in an average classroom that does not require any additional staffing or resources.

One advantage, among many others, is that as parents you do not have to pay much extra for your child to attend public school. Some extras might include special uniforms, art supplies, and in some cases additional books. School trips may also incur additional costs beyond the allocated budget and parents through fund-raisers and personal contributions often provide these funds. The cost is borne primarily by taxes although many school districts are now searching for other sources of funding to provide for some of the additional benefits made available to their students.

These extra benefits which schools are able to provide might range from special trips and activities, additional equipment and resources, access to community facilities and programs not covered by many school budgets. When cuts in programs have to be made due to decreased revenues, the choice is to either eliminate a program or find additional funding. Those programs might include more opportunities in the arts, music, drama and athletics as well as additional equipment and supplies in the realm of technology.

Because public schools are funded in large part by the local area where they exist, affluent suburban schools generally have more resources, better facilities and more well paid teachers than under financed urban school districts where many families live below the poverty level. A percentage of local taxes are allocated to public education and it makes sense that higher taxes provide more school revenue than an area where taxes are lower. This would also hold true for states as well as local judicatories where higher tax rates produce more income.

There are numerous families who have consciously decided to move their residence in order to be closer to a better public school. In addition, some school districts actually allow parents to make choices within the district and not be limited or constrained by geographical boundaries. You can easily find the public schools in your area whether by talking with neighbors and friends or calling your school district. Ways to evaluate your local, public school will be covered in the next chapter.

Magnet schools are another category of public schools attracting students with specific interests focused in a particular area. They might have programs that concentrate in science and technology, or in the fine and performing arts, or in international and global studies or they may exist to serve gifted and talented students. Regardless of their emphasis, magnet schools must still fulfill the regular academic requirements of the common core standards of public schools. What they offer is providing students an opportunity to pursue a special area of interest in depth and developing that to a higher level than might be possible in a regular, traditional public school.

NOTES:

Private Schools

Among the population of private schools there are different configurations, different philosophies and different histories and cultures. They vary according to the number of grade levels and there are many more private schools in the eastern part of the United States than in the midwest and west. There are both boarding and day schools, co-ed and single sex schools and schools that serve specifically defined populations from gifted to special needs students. Almost all of these schools charge tuitions that can range from a few thousand dollars to over $35,000 per year.

Private schools are sometimes referred to by some states as non-public schools, a term that is both unfortunate and undesirable. There are many different kinds of schools. The term "non-public" is a negative. By using *what you are not* to define you is much the same as being called "non-white" or a "non-believer". It would be far better to define something by what it is rather than using a majority to define a minority. It is as if you exist only as an extension or an appendage of the majority and have no identity of your own.

There are numerous private and independent schools including Catholic schools and other faith-based schools. These are often defined as holding close to a particular philosophy or ethos. Included are Montessori and Waldorf schools, some 700 Episcopal schools, boarding schools (some of which begin as early as the 7th grade), and special needs schools that address learning challenges as well as other obstacles faced by students that might prevent them from succeeding in a traditional school environment.

In the entire school population in the United States, approximately 10% of students attend what are defined as private schools. There are at least two types of private schools that include both independent schools and proprietary schools. These schools most often charge tuition to help cover the costs of educating their students and many of them offer scholarships to assist families who cannot afford to pay the full cost of the tuition. Private schools generally do not receive any public funding although there is some help from local governments with transportation and other limited resources such as textbooks. Private schools can also be selective about the students they accept and are sometimes limited because of how they are organized or configured.

Among the private schools are a wide variety of choices, including:

- Different grade level structures
- Single sex and co-ed schools
- Boarding schools, day schools and combinations of both
- Faith based schools, most of which are inclusive of multiple faiths
- Secular schools that do not emphasize any particular religion per se
- Proprietary schools that are owned by either individuals or a corporation
- Independent schools governed by a board of directors or trustees

There are many associations of these private schools including the National Association of Independent Schools that has some 1500 member schools. You can locate these schools, and others, through various state and regional associations or find them through an Internet search for private schools receiving more detailed information from their respective web sites. Many states have listings of private schools on their public education web sites as those schools must be registered and most often licensed by the state where they operate. This usually means that they have been accredited by a reputable organization. The challenge here is to choose which private school might serve your child best and why.

There are close to 31,000 private schools in the United States, serving over 5 million PK-12 students. Private schools account for 24% of the nation's schools and enroll just 10% of all PK-12 students. Most private school students, 80%, attend religiously affiliated schools. The majority of private schools are small, 86% have fewer than 300 students.

Because private schools generally charge tuition, it is often assumed that only wealthy people can afford to send their children to them and that most wealthy people do just that. The following data from February 2011, from the U.S. Census Bureau, on the social and economic characteristics of students enrolled in the nation's schools during the month of October 2009 refutes that assumption. Of the 8.5 million families with children in grades K-12 with annual incomes of $75,000 or more (the highest income bracket measured),

85% have children only in public schools and 12% have children only in private schools. Three percent have children in both types of schools.

The assumption that only people with high incomes can afford private schools is also not accurate in that many private schools provide scholarships for those students and families who cannot afford to pay the entire tuition. These scholarships are often based on financial need. School Scholarship Service in Princeton, New Jersey analyzes the financial statements of a family to determine how much assistance might be awarded.

There are advantages and disadvantages to private schools. Here are a few pluses and minuses to give you, as parents, an idea of what private schools offer, what many of them can do and in some cases what they cannot. It is not a case of private versus public but rather understanding why you might choose one rather than another. This is true in choosing between public or private and within each one of those categories as well as to type and kind of school.

After considering private schools you may wish to choose a public school. After considering public schools you may wish to choose a private school. Regardless of either choice, you still have choices within either category. This is the important point to remember. You are capable of making an informed choice, one that takes into account not only the needs and best interests of your child but also what a particular school offers. You want to choose the one that you believe has the best all around opportunities to help your child become a well-educated, happy and successful person.

What most private schools offer that they believe serve children well are small classes, individual attention, supportive and caring environments, enriched curriculums, committed and dedicated teachers and a partnership with parents, all designed to help children grow and develop appropriately. And, since private schools can be selective about which students are admitted, they have more control over their student populations.

It is not that public schools do not also offer many of these things but these are what the majority of private schools emphasize, sometimes more than grades, test scores and annual yearly progress reports.

Private schools are not burdened with public bureaucracies although they are, in most cases, accredited by reputable organizations. Neither do many private schools have the wide array of resources that public schools offer, often including well-developed and well-resourced athletic programs, extensive student support services, and larger student populations. Large schools are often able to provide a wide array of choices in programs, in teacher personalities and in a diversity of the student body.

Many, if not most, private schools have admissions criteria often based on academic and social standards. This means that private schools are not obligated to admit every student who applies. This selectivity has often give the impression of elitism because while you may wish to choose a private school, the private school must also desire to choose you or rather your child. Many private schools are committed to insuring a diverse student body thus overcoming some of the assumptions often expressed in the public arena.

NOTES:

Chapter Three

THE ASSESSMENT

Gathering information about a school can be much like a small research project. It can take awhile to assemble enough details so that you feel well informed. You want to have a complete and accurate picture of what the school is, what it does well, what its particular strengths and weaknesses are and what you can expect from your child's experience at the school whether it is for one year, four years or more.

Your sourcing of information might begin with a review of the school's web site as most schools today have one although they vary greatly in the amount of information you will find there. Some are fairly complete with the following list:

- Their history, mission and values stated clearly
- Names of faculty and staff, some include profiles
- Curriculum guides for various grade levels
- Lists of activities and special programs
- News and events
- Invitations to visit in person
- Their plans for the future

Other web sites are more limited and not so transparent. There are ways to evaluate any school through a systematic and thorough process, finding out what the pluses and minuses are of the place and information about the people who work there. Schools cannot be all things to all people and each one has its particular strengths as well as areas where they are not so strong. Keep in mind that you are looking for the school that is best for your child. You want the school where your child is going to connect well with the other people who are there and relate easily to what the program is that engages children. The school environment is a high priority.

Another source of information might be obtained through printed materials which the school has available for your review and which you can request be sent to you. You can read through these descriptions carefully, noting those things that you like, things that you might have further questions about and what you think could be missing that is important for you and your child.

The key factors of a good school are quality teachers, high and appropriate expectations for both students and adults, and the quality of the teaching/learning environment. Other components that are important are the resources available to help inspire students and their learning, and perhaps most importantly, the core values of the school and how they mesh with your own.

If possible and appropriate, be sure to interview the Principal, Head of School or at the least, the head of the division where your child will be spending a lot of time learning for the next several years. You may want to talk with the administrator who is in charge of hiring and evaluating teachers, who is responsible for the overall curriculum and the person who is most invested in the outcome for the students. This could be an assistant principal, a director of academic studies or someone other than the principal or head of the school.

The purpose of these interviews has several objectives. First, you want to find out what criteria are used to choose those people who will have the primary teaching/learning relationship with your child. Secondly, you want to know, beyond what you have read and heard, how the mission and philosophy of the school is enacted every day in the school community. What you are looking for is evidence that the learning environment is optimum for your child.

You may want to ask what the school has in place to provide students the necessary and sufficient support, encouragement and opportunities to develop their capacities to the highest levels. These would include academic, artistic, and athletic programs as well as how the school meets the cognitive, social, emotional, physical and spiritual needs of individual children. It's a tall order to be sure!

A list of questions for evaluating a school and for evaluating your choice of schools is included at the end of this book. Be sure to review those questions that have been developed by a number of parents who have already been through the process of choosing a school.

Talk with other parents whose children have attended or who are attending the school you are evaluating and see what their experiences have been or what they are currently. A note of caution here is that their children may or may not be like yours but if you are at this point in the process, the chances are that you have at least looked at what the school says it is and what it does and you have been sufficiently satisfied to continue exploring more in depth. Remember too, that there may well be more than one school that would be acceptable and appropriate for your child. In such cases, the final choice can be a challenge.

Schools as organizations can be looked at from several perspectives. You can see both form and function by looking at how the school is organized and whether it is a top down, hierarchical kind of organization or whether it is more democratic and participatory where there are signs of shared leadership and collaboration. You might prefer a school that is more structured and tightly organized or you might prefer one that is more relaxed and casual in its approach. Your preferences will usually coincide with your own values of what is important.

Culture and Climate

The atmosphere and attitudes that prevail in the school environment most often determine the climate in a school. You can tell fairly quickly whether that environment is generally positive, enthusiastic, energetic and encouraging or whether it is more on the dull, negative, punitive and restricted side of things. Obviously, you want your child in the former environment, not the latter one.

Some areas of a school and its programs will inevitably be stronger than others and other parts that may not be as well developed or emphasized. Much may depend on what the school has chosen to emphasize. What you must determine is which aspects of the school's culture are most important for your child and your family.

One parent who visited a school under consideration reported that the children did not seem to smile very much nor did they seem very animated or engaged with one another or their teachers. He reported he would not send his child to such a school even if it were the only one available. He would home school his child before choosing one that was less than acceptable.

There are reasons why a school appears the way it does and it would behoove you as a parent to get beyond the appearance to understand why the school feels one way as opposed to another. Try and discern why you are responding as you are.

An important part of school culture is how the school deals with different kinds of children and families. In other words, what are the school's position and practice with regard to what is often called the "Big Eight" social identifiers? Those characteristics by which many people are defined or described are: Ability (physical and mental), Age, Ethnicity, Gender, Race, Religion, and Sexual Orientation.

Diversity in our population today has become a major concern for many people. The Association of American Colleges and Universities defines diversity as "individual differences (e.g., personality, learning styles, and life experiences) and group/social differences (e.g., race/ethnicity, class, gender, sexual orientation, country of origin, and ability as well as cultural, political, religious, or other affiliations) that can be engaged in the service of learning" (AAC&U, 2009).

If social issues and social justice are important to you as a parent you want your child to be in a place that values these kinds of issues then you need to know how the school treats people who may have previously been marginalized in our society.

The following is one definition of social justice for your consideration. "We believe that social justice is both a process and a goal. The goal of social justice is full and equal participation of all groups in a society that is mutually shaped to meet their needs. Social justice includes a vision of society in which the distribution of resources is equitable and all members are physically and psychologically safe and secure. "(Adams, Bell & Griffin, 2007, p.1 in *Diversity Defined*). How a school measures up to that definition may help you in deciding where you want your child to spend some formative years.

John McKnight, an author and researcher, has written a number of articles on the subject of building an inclusive community. McKnight is Emeritus Professor of Education and Social Policy and co-director of the Asset-Based Community Development Institute at Northwestern University. He is the coauthor of *Building Communities from the Inside Out* and the author of *The Careless Society*. If you are particularly interested in this subject you may want to review some of his work.

Culture is the way the school thinks about itself and the way that it acts as a community. With this definition in mind you can see the importance of school culture and climate and how those impact and influence the overall school program including academics, athletics and the arts.

A school's culture might also be defined as coming from its beliefs about itself, how it regards the people who work there, both students and adults, as well as how it embraces different kinds of families who are part of the school because they send their children to that particular place.

A school, much like an individual, has a distinct personality that is seen and felt by its behavior, by its reputation and by how people in the community regard it. A school is an active, organic and dynamic institution, not a static and stationary entity and to the extent that the school is both comfortable and confident within itself, very much like a human being. The school will be attractive and appealing or it will be a place you want to avoid. Conversely, a school might be unsure of its identity and in the process of working through some defining issues of what it wants to be. In that case you could either want to be part of helping that process or you may not want to participate in that experience. In either case, you have a fairly clear choice. As you know, it is not always as easy as choosing black or white but often shades of gray!

Very few schools may have everything you seek for your child. Your objective should be to get as close to the ideal or optimum as possible, knowing that you may have to compromise somewhere on your list of expectations. As an institution made up of imperfect human beings, there is no such thing as a "perfect" school. There are however, those that are more appropriate than others and you need to use your own measures, or even those of others, in order to determine your final choice.

The choices may boil down to two or three distinct possibilities and then your task is to put them side by side and make some comparisons as to which of the few "finalists" are the most appealing and why. Think about several years and what your hopes are for your child over the next few years of his or her life in terms of growth and developing potential. The name of the game at this point is expanding your child's world of learning.

NOTES:

Chapter Four

CHANGING SCHOOLS

There are natural points along the way when a child moves from one stage to another and this may be a time for changing schools. If your child has been attending a pre-school, a stand-alone school organized to serve your child's developmental growth from about age 2 or 3 to age 5, then you must look for the next school experience, probably beginning in either Kindergarten or Grade 1.

In some communities, it is an easy transition and the flow goes from one place to another almost seamlessly. In a few situations, there are elementary schools that have a pre-school as part of their program so there is no need for a change but those schools are generally the exception rather than the prevailing norm.

The time for a change is an opportunity to review the possible choices rather than just follow the crowd or take the most convenient option. Taking the necessary time to make the change may mean starting to consider the next school early rather than waiting until near the end of the current year. In the private school world, for example, the admissions process for the following year begins as early as the fall of the current year, with decisions being made by the school in March or April for enrollment in the fall. Talk to the school to understand their requirements and their timetables.

A word of caution here is how and when to let your current school know that you are contemplating a change, especially if the school assumes you will automatically be enrolling for the following year. Public schools that "lose" children also lose the funding associated with the student. The same is true for private schools that receive tuition. In either case you will eventually need to tell the school you are leaving because you will need your child's records sent to the next school. Timing could be critical and waiting to inform your current school may the better strategy.

Other reasons for making a change in schools, in addition to a natural ending in one place and a new beginning elsewhere, may include the need to change residences and moving to a different community. In such an event you will want to gather information ahead of the move if at all possible and conduct your research and due diligence before arriving at your new residence. You might even decide to live in one area rather than another because of the school which your child will attend.

The way many schools are organized can also make a transition easier at certain grade levels. For example, ending an elementary school and starting a middle school is a reasonable break in the developmental scale. A similar situation prevails with the change from middle school to high school. The specific grade levels may vary with the school and the community but the schools will usually be configured somewhat the same although in different neighborhoods within a larger geographical area.

Changing schools can be a challenge for children in that they often feel like they are leaving the known for the unknown. They may also have made good friends and feel like they are losing those connections. If the change comes at one of those "natural" breaks, the explanation for the change is easier. If there is a physical move from one place to another, change is a given. Children are sometimes more resilient than we think.

One way to make the change more comfortable is to let the child know this is happening and not make the announcement ex post facto. Like many life changes, gradual is often better than sudden. You can also put the change in the context of other changes, such as those your child is experiencing such as losing teeth, getting taller, and adding more learning experiences and more knowledge every year. It is all about growth and change!

One of the most important points about change is that *planned* change is better and more desirable than unplanned change. The dynamics of planned change require some careful thought, time given to the process and professional help from someone who specializes in school placement if you need it. You can often find these people in the yellow pages or on the web under school counselors or placement counselors.

In the later years, a change may be indicated because of a need for some kind or program or activity that may not be available in your child's current school. If the current school does not offer advanced studies or a well resourced athletic or arts program and your child has a special interest in one of those areas, then it might behoove you to find a school that is well regarded for offerings that will engage your child at a different level.

In another scenario, your child may experience his or her current school as too challenging or too uncomfortable for whatever reasons. The school and your child may not be a good fit academically or socially and to continue trying to change the child to fit the school may not be the best strategy. The school is unlikely to change to fit the child unless it is something within the school structure or program that can be dealt with effectively and resolved easily. One example could be a schedule change or a course selection change as those can be dealt with more easily than something much larger such as a specific teacher mismatch.

There are also times when a child may want to change to avoid dealing with a conflict. It might be better for the child to learn how to resolve a difference rather than to find an easy out. In other words, that kind of learning experience may be as valuable as any other in the school environment.

NOTES:

CONCLUSIONS

There are many iterations of different kinds of schools It is even possible to find one K-12 school in one building, probably a small school or such a school in several buildings on one campus, probably a larger school. You can find a stand-alone school of just a few grades –a pre-school, elementary or middle or secondary school. There are a myriad of choices. There are public schools, charter schools, magnet schools, private schools, many of which have some stated religious connection and many that do not. There are private, independent schools which are purely secular that have strong values and a clearly stated mission and purpose. You want to choose a school that you believe will serve your child's learning needs and interests in the most complete way.

What you want is a happy, engaged, enthusiastic child, one who is having an enjoyable and positive learning experience overall. There will be inevitable bumps in the road and these can usually be negotiated without a major catastrophe. Your objective in finding the best, most appropriate school for your child is worth your investment of time, energy and effort to the extent that is both reasonable and realistic.

One of the major factors to keep in mind is your sense of the character and quality of the adults in your child's school environment. To the extent that they obviously love what they are doing and they appear to be talented, dedicated and committed to their students and their profession, there is a greater likelihood for a happy learner.

While the physical environment of any school is important, the social and academic environments are also of great value as they add greatly (or not) to your child's educational experience. Remember that learning accumulates over time and a long-term view of several years is better than making a snap judgment based on one experience.

This questionnaire is provided to assist you in evaluating your school choices. Answering these questions will help give you a guide for choosing the best school for your child.

Questions for Parents in Choosing the "Best" School for your Child

1. To the extent you know your child (children) and their personalities, what are the top five things you would look for in choosing a school?

2. What would you want to avoid in choosing a school?

3. How would you rank each of the following in terms of their importance on a scale of 1-5, five being the most important?
   a- Quality of teachers
   b- Curriculum or programs of the school.
   c- School's physical environment
   d- School's commitment to ethics and character education

e- Leadership of the school.
f- Philosophy and values of the school
g- Size of school and size of classes
h- Location of the school.
i- Reputation of the school according to other parents
j- Type of student body, diverse vs. homogeneous
k- Athletic program and choices
l- Student support for different learning styles

4. What would cause you to think about changing schools?

5. How satisfied are you with the school where your children are now on a scale of 1-5, five being the most satisfied? Why?

6. What kinds of things did you consider when you chose your current school?

7. If you were doing it all over again, is there anything you would do differently and if so, what?

8. What do you hope will be the outcome of your child's education at the end of grade five or six?

   At the end of grade eight or nine?

   Upon graduation from high school?

9. With attendance at a college, university or post-secondary educational experience presumed, what criteria will you help to influence in your child's selection of possible choices?

10. Would you consider a bridge year between high school and college? Why or Why not?

If you would like help and some professional counsel in choosing a school, you may contact the author of this book through his web site: garygruber.com

Good luck and best wishes for you and your children for a most happy and successful school experience. There is no greater investment you can make that is more important than the education of your children.

NOTES:

Acknowledgments

Thanks to all those teachers and school leaders who work diligently every day to give children the best possible learning opportunities. They are talented, dedicated and committed professional educators. They have chosen their life's work because they are caring and compassionate men and women whose best work often gets lost in the shuffle. We hold them up here as exemplary human beings who deserve to be recognized and appreciated for their efforts and accomplishments.

Thanks to my many colleagues over the years with whom I had the privilege of working with to create schools and learning experiences for both students and adults. You made my work more meaningful, enjoyable and rewarding than I could ever have imagined.

Thanks to my editor, best friend, co-pilot and soul mate, Susan Richardson, who keeps me to the task of writing and does not settle until we get it right. Her insistence on clarity and detail makes all that I do so much better.

www.ingramcontent.com/pod-product-compliance
Lightning Source LLC
Chambersburg PA
CBHW060621070426
42447CB00040B/2241